Raclette Living

M.K. O'Hara

ISBN:1519766637
ISBN-13:9781519766632

DEDICATION

For John

CONTENTS

ACKNOWLEDGMENTS

I would like to thank everyone who has gathered at my table to share in the raclette dinner events.   Thanks also to Kirstie Pearson, Val and Ray Bostrom for turning me on to the crazy fun…..

THE BASICS

Base requirements for 8 person raclette:

 Equipment and food to cook

Raclette Equipment

Raclette Kit (should contain coupelles, scrapers, and the raclette grill).   The Raclette grill comes in different sizes. I've seen 2 to 8 person grills.   I own 8 person grills myself.

Power: dedicated circuit (in my experience, if you have whacky 1952 electrics going on like I do, you'll pop a circuit sometime during dinner if you don't test first. ;-(

Fondue forks

Basting brush (to baste the top of the grill with canola oil)

Small bowl of canola oil for re-oiling the grill top as needed.

Raclette Food

- Canola oil (this has a higher smoke point than olive oil)
- Dipping sauces in bowls or bottles - catsup, mustards, soy, Worcestershire, hot sauce, chili, etc.
- 2 lbs red potatoes boiled to *almost* done, cooled and sliced thin
- 2 thinly sliced zucchini or yellow squash
- 1 jar of gherkin pickles (the little ones the size of a pinky finger)
- 1 lb. mushroom slices
- 2 lbs chicken boneless and skinless chicken breast cut into 1 inch cubes
- 2 lbs sirloin steak cut into 1 inch cubes
- 1 lb. small to medium shrimp
- 3 types of cheese (this can change based on *your* main meal theme)
  - Cheddar (sliced or shredded)

- ○ Swiss (sliced or shredded)
- ○ Mozzarella (sliced or shredded)

Your preferences will be different from mine and as you do this more and more, you'll find the grocery list changes based on the theme of the party.   If you find the recipes in the back of this book something you'll use right away, make sure to add those ingredients to your grocery list!

THE HISTORY AND BACKGROUND OF RACLETTE

Raclette has been around as far back as the 13th century. In French, it means to scrape, which is the traditional method used in Europe and modified just a bit for us here. Raclette today involves an electric table-top grill with small handled pans called coupelles.   The coupelles sit beneath a heating element that is topped by a metal plate or stone.

Cheese is heated to melting and served over meat or vegetables.   Traditionally, the melting happens dangerously close to an open fire with a huge chunk of cheese. When the cheese reaches its peak of melted deliciousness, it is then scraped onto a chunk of bread. Well, if you are in the fields of Switzerland or Germany you can do it that way. This is where we part ways with tradition and give it the modern, urban twist enjoyed today.

Today, food is cooked on the top plate of the grill, and then cheese is melted in the coupelle and scraped onto the food. Often times, cooked food is placed in the coupelle, topped with cheese and then set under the heating element until the cheese reaches that gooey deliciousness we have grown to love.

Some of the lessons I have learned over time is to delegate the foods out to the attendees...it gets them into the mood for the event weeks in advance. It builds excitement and also offers new and unique perspectives to what pairings can be created. The taco recipe was an idea from one of the usual suspects. Follow up a couple days before to make sure no one forgets their assigned food.

I might remind you not to try EVOO (extra virgin olive oil) once again due to the smoke point. The grill gets super hot and you will have that oily veil hanging in the air and attaching itself to your draperies for the time to come. And, an overly-sensitive smoke detector might just go off which makes it very hard to have a decent dinner conversation.

Try to make sure that your electrical circuit really is set up to handle the job. There is no shame in running an orange extension cord into the next room to make sure of this, as long as you have warned everyone within earshot to mind the cord.

The question of how do handle more than 8 people at a table? You can pair up couples to share a coupelle leaving it to them to determine who is managing the goey concoctions of deliciousness that might arise from the cozy situation.

THE RACLETTE DINNER

The size of your raclette dish dictates the number of folks you can have at the party. My raclette is an 8 person, so we manage to all gather around the raclette.   Make sure your dining table can adequately allow for seating and reaching. Be aware that the grill gets VERY HOT so reaching across the grill should be done with care in mind. This turns into a boarding house reach party if everyone turns their own food.   We normally have one person in charge of turning the beef, one person in charge of the chicken and shrimp and veg.

My usual guests are well trained in the raclette experience. We have turned this into pot luck where the grocery list is divided between us, and each person brings enough to serve 8.

Inviting newbies to the table is as much fun for the usual suspects as it is for the newbies. Pair up a newbie with a seasoned diner and you will find that to be the easiest way to manage the table. Rather than trying to do it all yourself, try delegating and enjoying the experience yourself. People like helping out since raclette is such an off the beaten path experience.

What you'll need for a basic Raclette dinner:

Invitations for your friends who enjoy non-traditional adventures in dining.

Food (see the list)

Prepare the food as per the list.

Equipment (see the list and test that outlet you're going to be using)

The grill takes about 10 minutes to come to temperature, so this is a good time for cocktails and seating arrangements to be sorted out.

Take a slight amount of canola oil and coat the top plate of the Raclette grill.

Each guest should have one coupelle, a fondue fork, a table fork and spoon.

Gather around the grill.

Cook the meats on the grill top until done. Remove to share

on plates and add more to keep the food going.   This part of dinner takes some time to get used to. There is an initial unnerving push to hurry things along and *this is the beauty of raclette* -- You can't hurry it. Raclette forces you to slow down, relax and enjoy conversation with your fellow diners. So, relax, enjoy the food and the experience.

As dinner progresses, allow your diners to understand they are free to construct their own meals. Their coupelles are used to create their own specific little pans of delicious food.   I suggest you get feedback and ideas for the next time, since there is always a next time.

DINNER THEMES

A dinner theme? You say! Yes, it can happen.   You can have any or all of the following and then some:

- Birthday

- Anniversary

- Memorial Day

- Cold Winter Night

- Mystery Dinner

- Bad Art Night

- Usual Suspects

- Newbies only

- Raclette for Two

- Raclette for Ten

RACLETTE RECIPES

Coupelle Tacos

- Bag of "dipping" tortillas
- <u>Cooked </u>ground beef seasoned with taco spices
- Shredded cheese
- Salsa
- Sour cream

Place one dipping tortilla in the coupelle.   Scoop in ground beef, layer with shredded cheese. Place coupelle under heating element until the cheese is melted.   Remove onto plate, top with salsa and sour cream.

Coupelle S'mores
- Graham crackers
- Chocolate chip morsels
- Mini marshmallows

Place cracker in the bottom of the coupelle. Cover with six chocolate chips and a few mini marshmallows. Place coupelle under heating element AND PAY CLOSE ATTENTION TO THE MARSHMALLOW as they rise quickly and may reach the heating element. Remove onto plate, let cool and enjoy.

Coupelle Cheesy Potatoes
- Cooked potato slices
- Cheddar cheese (sliced or shredded)
- Chives
- Sour cream

Layer the coupelle base with sliced potato. Cover with cheddar cheese and place under the heating element. When the cheese is melted, remove onto place, top with sour cream and chives.

Coupelle Pizza
- Buttermilk biscuits in the can
- Your choice of cheese (shredded)
- Your choice of toppings (cooked meat, olives, etc.)
- Italian spices (ex: oregano, basil, etc.)

Layer the coupelle base with a sliver of part of one of the buttermilk biscuits. Just a sliver, not the entire biscuit. Poke a few holes in the dough with a fork and let this cook until it has cooked through and is lightly browned. Add cheese and your spice and toppings and place back under heat until cheese has melted. When the cheese is melted, remove onto plate.

RACLETTE LIVING

ABOUT THE AUTHOR

MK OHara has been enjoying raclette dining with friends and family for nearly a decade. The author resides in Illinois.

10247072R00016

Made in the USA
Monee, IL
24 August 2019